Ny'

CW00556456

The princ

here although explained

for business will be

good for you to study even

at your age.

Kat[signature]

2018

Karl George qualified in industry as a Chartered Certified Accountant in 1991. He started the development of his presentation skills as a lecturer and trainer of accountants having studied NLP and accelerated learning techniques. Karl has a proven track record of working for the overall benefit of enterprises in the owner-managed business sector and also works with numerous other enterprises in the public sector. He is a sought after business consultant, presenter and author specialising in soft-skills – namely business strategy, people and systems development and executive coaching. He inspires his audiences with his passionate delivery and depth of subject knowledge.

Karl is well known in the local community and managing director of Andersons KBS Limited. Andersons KBS is a multi-disciplined Business Consultancy and Accountancy Firm specialising in business development services to owner-managed business and public sector organisations. It is located in the heart of the financial community in Birmingham City Centre and employs 25 people.

Karl has been recognised for his contribution to the business community and his own business success with numerous awards and accolades. For example:-

Carlton TV's Young Business Midlander of the Year

Birmingham's Young Professional of the Year

Black Business in Birmingham's Achiever of the Year

Giving back is an important philosophy that Karl lives by and makes time to contribute to a number of business and community initiatives. These include:-

Council Member of Chamber of Commerce

President of 100 Black Men of Birmingham

Chair of African Caribbean Business Forum

Member of Carlton Television's Diversity Panel

Member of Financial and Advisory Skills Task Force

Karl George

Most people only try

I make sure

Design: Kiwi, Birmingham

Andersons KBS Ltd, Birmingham

www.andersonskbs.com

Published by

Andersons KBS Ltd

The Old Guild House

One New Market Street

Birmingham

B3 2NH

First published in 2003

Printed in England by Louis Drapkin Ltd, Birmingham

ISBN 0-9544896-0-8

Most people only try

I make sure

Simple strategies to help you achieve business success.

If you have been in business for some time, you will find techniques, information and exercises that will help you to develop.

If you are starting a business, this book will help you to deploy specific strategies that will pave the way for successful development.

Dedications

My God

My Grandmother - she told me I was going to be an accountant

My parents

My co-directors; Michael Green, Ralph Rowledge, Mark Howell

The support team at Andersons KBS, especially Lisa Smith

Clyde Pile - my first mentor

Adrian Leedham and all the team at George Leedham

Ian Fletcher and the team at 2020 Consulting Group

Peter Murray - my first consulting client

Fred Rose - my karate instructor

RAN One Consulting Group

My clients

My supporters

Karl George FCCA

At the age of 14 the author was the manager and a dancer in the Wild Flash Crew break dance company. The company was featured in a Central Television Documentary and performed throughout the Midlands.

Two years later he was running several successful karate schools across Birmingham. He became a Black Belt in the sport at the age of 18.

When 23, he qualified as an accountant and a year later started his own business.

He is married to Judy and has 3 sons.

Foreword

Those of us who know Karl George, know that he has that winning combination of determination and enormous enthusiasm. This comes across in the book.

We all know that many business books simply contain common sense and this one is no exception but it is packaged in a very user-friendly and readable way so that you do not need an MBA to understand it.

It will make an invaluable contribution to those contemplating starting their own business and many business people who read the book will be thankful subsequently that they did, bearing in mind the high failure rate for small businesses.

John H Pratt
President Birmingham Chamber of Commerce
Partner Pinsent Curtis Biddle

Contents

Introduction

Business is simple

That is a bold statement to make when statistics show that approaching 90% of new businesses fail within ten years.

So, how can I possibly justify saying that 'business is simple', when more than eight out of ten start-ups fail inside a decade?

I can justify saying it because I know that the important rules of business are simple.

In the following pages, I will show you just how simple, and give you seven tried and tested steps that, if taken, will increase dramatically your chances of success.

Join me on a voyage of discovery.

Simple does not mean easy

A great deal of hard work is required to create a successful business. True, if you have a passion for what you do and work intelligently, it will feel less hard. However, on the bottom line it is still hard; but it is simple.

I know that it is not difficult because in my various capacities as accountant, business advisor, lecturer and trainer I have had exposure to countless businesses and the people who run them. Through this, I have been able to identify seven underlying mechanisms and the strategies for implementing them that will always help to create success and sustain it.

They have delivered for generations of business people. They have delivered success for me. They can deliver it for you.

My story

I started in business in 1992. I had qualified as a chartered certified accountant. Almost immediately, I was made redundant when the firm I was with was bought by a substantial plc. It turned out to be a blessing in disguise when the new business asked me to help them in a consultative capacity as they implemented their new plans. I had always had a passion for business and this work gave me a taste for controlling my own destiny. I decided to remain independent. So, the newly qualified accountant started an accounting practice in a makeshift office in his mother's house. I had no money. I had scant experience. I was just 24.

Over the years, I have progressed to employing scores of people. On the way I have experienced a period, when turnover doubled every year for four years and I have steered my company into the top twenty percent, in terms of size of accountancy practices.

Walking the talk

I have had offices in the most prestigious and sought after locations.

I have shared the stage in my speaking career with international speakers and best selling authors.

I have seen business associates become millionaires by creating businesses that have benefited from the internet-boom.

I have consulted for businesses and individuals that have lost it all, and built it all back.

I have lost it all, started again and developed a stronger business therefore.

Along the way, I have helped clients to break important barriers, like the £1million turnover threshold, profitably, and with cash in the bank.

"Success leaves clues"

The title above is a quotation from an early inspiration of mine, Anthony Robbins. It impressed me when I first read it, and as time has gone by, I have come to realise just how true it is. All successful businesses leave clear clues.

I have diligently studied those clues. They have helped me to identify and name the seven strategies that you will learn about in this book. In turn, they led me to coin a phrase that encapsulates them all:

Most people only try. I make sure.

What it means is; successful business owners do not just give it their best shot. They do whatever it takes to make sure. As simple as it sounds, this is what sets them apart from other people. They are not the 90% who started a business and failed.

They are the 10% who are still in business.

Analyse the reality and picture the ideal

A careful analysis of the needs of the marketplace and your strengths and weaknesses will help you identify precisely where your business is.

Knowing where you are starting from is an essential element in planning any journey.

Equally important is to know where you are going. To know this it is necessary to picture your ideal business structure and what you want from life as an individual. You will quickly realise that the two are inextricable.

Analysing the reality and structuring the vision will enable you to identify your unique strengths and how you can develop them to increase the chances of success.

The significant difference

There is a real difference between a current reality and a vision. The moment at which there is understanding of the former and identification of the latter is a very important one.

Even more important is the fact that although all businesses are faced with reality, even if they fail to understand or analyse it, almost none has a vision.

Lack of a vision constrains most small and medium sized businesses. Once there is a vision the road ahead can be mapped and the factors critical to a successful journey can be identified. This is like any other journey. If you know where you are going you can identify the turnings, forks along the way, and make the right decisions.

Identify the steps

Another advantage of analysing the present and structuring the vision means that it is possible to identify the changes that are necessary. Equally, it is valuable for identifying things that should not be changed.

Knowing where you are going means that operational plans can be made which implement the fundamental changes necessary to achieve the vision.

It will work because behind everything you do will be a powerful, enthusiastic and determined entrepreneur…you. You will be powerful, enthusiastic and determined because you will come to realise why it is important to satisfy your needs, while learning new skills and how doing these things simultaneously will increase your profits, bank balance and ultimately improve your lifestyle.

Work on your business. Not in it.

As we identify new strategies and ways of operating change, keep in mind one of the essential objectives identified by the business guru, Michael Gerber.

One of our essential objectives, he maintained, was to work **on** our business rather than **in** our business.

Key to making this shift of focus is the recognition that, in order to do it, we must have documented systems and procedures for every essential function in the business.

In other words, the owner should not have to be there to make sure. He must make sure that others can make sure. This working **on** and not **in** must inform every decision.

Developing the organisational structure, and the key responsibilities for each post in the business, will have a far greater long-term impact on the business than expending energy doing everything yourself.

Many owner managers object, saying that they have no time to implement the necessary systems. This means they are caught in what looks to them like a Catch 22 situation. It is not a Catch 22 situation because it is resolvable. As soon as you begin to find the time, it releases more time. Finding that first tranche of time, no matter how difficult it seems, is vital because without it there will never be the payback - which is the time to enjoy all the gifts that life can offer.

Ordinary people - extraordinary results

The ultimate business model includes not only efficient systems but also good people. These can be defined as ordinary people who produce extraordinary results. You might think that they are in short supply. They are not.

Getting extraordinary results from ordinary people is easy if you can surround value-based work practices with a culture of fun.

We spend a large proportion of our waking hours at work. It is natural that human beings need to feel that they are valued in an activity which consumes such a large part of their conscious hours.

It is an employer's obligation to fulfill these two objectives but the amazing thing is that the employer who goes further and adds fun will get extraordinary results.

The Seven Strategies

Motivation

Positive Set

Organisation

Technique

Investment

Mentoring

Self

All the case histories that preface the seven sections are based on real clients or friends of the author. He wishes to thank them for their permission to use the information

1 | Motivation

The partners in a security and alarm company set up their own business to pursue their dream of self-employment. They wanted to be answerable to no-one, control their own destiny and reap financial rewards.

However, success did not come over night. It has taken ten years for them to realise their dream and create a multi-million pound business.

On day one, the partners understood their industry but lacked broader business skills. This slowed their growth and meant it took them longer than originally planned to leave behind the low salary that comes with a start-up business. Some days it must have felt as if they had made a big mistake. So what kept them going?

Motivation.

They were driven forward by their desire to create a successful, standard setting company and to reap the financial rewards they wanted.

This chapter will make sure you can reap the rewards of focused motivation.

Motivation

"A journey of a thousand miles starts with a single step."

Remember, motivation follows action. There will be times when you do not feel like doing what you know is essential to success. However, just start - because once you do, the motivation will follow.

Successful entrepreneurs I have studied have all demonstrated strong motivation. A key factor has been the ability to align their personal ambitions with those of their business. This is effective because we are all motivated by pleasure. The linking of pleasurable outcomes with business goals is what drives these people.

What they have done is create a mental picture of the business that they want. This picture is fine-tuned and developed through time, but it is always in focus.

The resulting motivation is such that these people will also do almost anything to avoid failure. This drives a dogmatic persistence. They know what they want. Equally important, they know what they do not want.

Pleasure and pain

It is a fact that short-term pleasure tends to lead to long-term pain. The converse is also true; short-term pain tends to lead long-term pleasure. The sooner we recognise this, the sooner we can use it to help our motivation.

Business owners have to put in a lot of front-end hard work. Recognising its value, and the rewards it will lead to, is very important. It is true of start-up situations and long-established businesses, which have not developed their full potential.

Focusing on the long-term goals, including the pleasures of success, generates the motivation to do the initial hard work.

Encouragingly, the greater the initial effort, the greater the eventual success.

Exercise

You can develop your motivational quotient by deciding exactly what it is you want out of life and equally importantly, what you do not want. It is important that you write down your choices. Spend some time now and make some notes.

The power questions, which follow, may help you to define your answers. Take your time, work through them and answer truthfully. Review all your answers by reading them all through at one go. You will probably be surprised at what you discover about yourself.

Power Questions

1. What are the five things that you value most in your life?
2. What are the three most important goals in your life?
3. What would you do if you won a million pounds?
4. What would you do if you had no physical or mental limitations?
5. What would you do with your life if you only had six months to live?
6. What have you always wanted to do, but been afraid to attempt?
7. Looking back over all the things you have done, what has made you feel most important?
8. If you could be granted one wish, what would it be?
9. What would you do if you knew that you could not fail?
10. What is the major purpose in your life?
11. What are your strengths? List three.
12. What are your weaknesses? List three.
13. If you could be granted one skill or ability, what would it be?
    For example: the ability to speak a language, paint, play music, be a good tennis player.
14. What gives you the greatest pleasure and satisfaction in your life?
15. What legacy would you like to leave?
16. What three things have you been putting off that would enable you to get your affairs in order?
17. In your ideal life, how often would you pray to and worship God?
18. If you chose your food on nutritional value, what items that you currently eat would you eliminate?
19. Who is living the life you admire?
20. Describe what you think it is like to live that life?
21. Who is doing the kind of work you wish to do?
22. Imagine you are very old and a child asks, "What are you most proud of about your life?" What do you answer?
23. Your life has resulted in three things changing in the world. What are they?

Journal

Here is a great piece of advice. The journey is more important than the arrival at any destination. In fact, there is no 'arrival' because there is always further to go. The journey is all-important and is itself the success. It is essential you record it. Start a journal. It is one of the most significant actions you will ever take.

Create your journal

1. Decide what sort of book or folder it will be written in. Choose carefully, make it special and personalise it.

2. Gather all the information that you have been working on relevant to your goal-setting and personal development. Arrange it by category and chronologically.

3. Record items on a regular basis. Choose seven to ten categories. (E.g. health, spirituality, finance, diet, goals, diary, adventure, children, love, quotes, dreams)

4. Create and label sections for inspirational poems or pictures. It is very important that you personalise the journal.

5. Use your journal to record your goals. Evaluate on a regular basis where you are, to make sure you are on the right track.

Painting the picture

In your journal, describe exactly what you want for your business and what it will look like when it is finished.

Of course, you will have to ensure that your personal goals align with your business goals. Write these down in detail. You may be clear about what you want but you give your ideas real power when you write them down. If there is more than one business owner, then you all need to agree on the picture. (You could put this in the business section of your journal).

Some valuable words by Calvin Coolidge

The words below encapsulate for me why successful businesses are successful…and why their owners are motivated to continue working through all types of adversity, loneliness, pressure and heartache.

"Press on.
Nothing can take the place of persistence.
Talent will not; the world is full of unsuccessful people with talent.
Genius will not; unrewarded genius is almost a proverb.
Education alone will not; the world is full of educated derelicts.
Persistence and determination alone are omnipotent."

It is not only important that the owner manager is motivated; they must also be able to motivate the team. This is a key ingredient of leadership. Every business needs **one** identifiable leader. This leader must have the ability to take their team on the journey of success that is in the leader's mind.

Aspects of leadership

The leader's vision must have been developed via consultations with all the stakeholders and then articulated clearly, concisely and regularly. The leader needs to pick his team to ensure the success of his plans. He needs to support and motivate everyone who is involved in achieving the plan.

Leadership is based on two things:

1. Understanding the motivation of the people who work for you.
2. Being able to get them to work towards the vision of where the business is going.

Anyone who is not working towards the vision must be removed for the benefit of the team. This is true whether it is a result of incompetence or non-conformance. The effect on the business is exactly the same; it is not working to its full potential.

Leaders must remember that people will be influenced by a leader's actions rather than what they say. Words and actions must be congruent.

Many of the businesses that I have worked with have not had a clear leader. In many instances, even though someone has been identified as a leader, the function has not been understood properly and therefore not discharged correctly.

The results of inadequate leadership can be severely damaging and are significant drivers of the following:

- 40% of businesses fail within 1 year
- 80% of businesses fail within 5 years
- Owner managers spend most of their time working in their business as opposed to on their business.
- Businesses continually make bad and costly decisions.
- Owner managers are continually complaining about performance of co-directors/ partners and employees.
- Most small businesses are undercapitalised

Effective leadership is the key to remedying all of the preceding problems.

At this point there will be readers who are thinking:

"I am the boss and I know what I am doing and these things are still happening to my business."

I would answer saying:

"I agree you are the boss. Are you, though, an effective leader?"

The following analogy will be helpful.

Who is really responsible for the success of a Premiership football team? Is it the individual talent of one of their star players? Is it about collecting a pool of talented players and letting them perform? Does the pitch they play on, or the training they do, have an impact?

It is possible to point to examples where teams have had a star talent playing in a pool of other recognised talent with excellent facilities and coaching and yet have been relegated.

The truth is, that all the above factors can have something to contribute to success, but when the team fails to perform it is clear leadership which is lacking.

A team needs a good manager who looks at the bigger picture supported by a good captain who can help the detailed implementation on the field.

In business the same principles apply. We need star employees, excellent procedures, systems, technology and machinery but without effective leadership the potential will never be fulfilled. Without leadership failure is a simple matter of 'when' not 'if'. Imagine a football team without a manager or a captain.

The football manager who doesn't manage is directly comparable with the business boss who doesn't lead. It is a source of wonder and bafflement why many people enter the world of entrepreneurship and growing a business without developing the time, skill and resources to perform effectively in the critical role of leader. The reason they do not is usually because they do not recognise how crucial leadership is until it is too late. Recognition of the importance of the role can be like a smack in the face. It is that obvious. However, many still have no idea that they do not possess the skills to be effective. It is hard to find these skills and bring them in and equally hard to develop them in the self, particularly if there is no knowledge of the scale and scope of the skills. We cannot know what we do not know.

In recent years I have had the opportunity to lead many organisations and businesses in the last decade and to interact with other leaders. I have come to the conclusion that leadership is not difficult and follows some basic guidelines. By following them you can dramatically improve the efficiency of your business.

Below are listed seven actions that, if taken, will improve the quality of your leadership, and can be implemented immediately.

To be effective they must be implemented in the order in which they are presented here.

1. Strategy

Know where you are going and why. Be sure that where you are heading is a real and achievable goal identified by real research and commitment to detail. Your conviction for the goal must be unquestionable. Everyone will be relying on you for the passion, driven by the vision, if things do not go to plan.

(Later on in the chapter there is advice on creating a strategic plan and how important it is to communicate it.)

2. Single Out

Add detail to the vision. The clarity this will create establishes you as the leader. It also defines the roles and responsibilities of others and how the leader will lead. It will entail implementation detail and deciding on the type of people and resources you need. There will also need to be contingency plans for shortfalls or failure of aspects because it is important for the leader to be one step ahead of the game, able to anticipate problems and have a plan for dealing with them. This can only come about by developing detailed action plans that ultimately refer back to strategy. A detailed organisational structure must be designed which embodies all functional responsibilities in all key areas like sales and marketing, finance, administration etc.

3. Success Monitoring

Decide which parameters and functions can be monitored regularly to determine whether the overall business is moving in the right direction. It is also very important to know what the alternatives will be if things are not going to plan.

It is impossible to anticipate every scenario but providing the key indicators are well-chosen, decisions can always be taken to optimise any contingent situation.

By reviewing the strategic objectives, measurement criteria can be broken down into sequential elements. For example, if annual turnover of £3m is forecast for year 3 with growth of £1m in years 1, 2 and 3 be sure that these numbers are achievable and based on real research and commitment to detail. Your belief in, and commitment to the end goal, must be unquestionable.

It is also possible to deduce the anticipated turnover for each month of the projection. This can then be further deconstructed into the number of sales presentations to be made, contacts established and so on. By monitoring the number of contacts made per month we can take action immediately if it is below expectations.

4. Structure

We have now identified our strategy and implementation details including items we should monitor consistently to make sure we are on track.

The next step is more problematic because it is practical rather than theoretical. We need to manage the process.

This is the point at which other people, co-directors and/or employees do not carry out their tasks. This is the stage where colleagues turn up to meetings without preparing reports or completing tasks set. This is where it can all go wrong.

Solution:

Schedule all meeting dates for the 12 months forward.

Decide on the reporting structure and align it with the previously identified success monitors.

Rationale - leaders fail sometimes because team members know tasks will be **set** but not **appraised**. They do not get (or expect) praise for achieving targets and the remuneration and bonus structures are not linked to achieving company objectives.

Weekly stand-up meetings can be planned with whole departments, or if practicable the whole company. Focus group meetings with functional managers can be held monthly. It is important to identify structures for each meeting and to carefully plan the agenda.

5. Style

Now it is possible to work with the whole company to achieve objectives and there is a benchmark for checking progress on a monthly basis.

Leadership style is next. This involves deciding how you are going to maintain records of all the tasks and responsibilities set for every individual. The motivation, support, encouragement and coercion required by each and every person to achieve their objectives will require the use of different skills and communications channels. These are as wide ranging as formal conversation, memo, informed chat, written warning, a bonus or present, an encouraging smile…

It is vital that the leader's own work is managed and delegated effectively. This may mean relying on the strengths of others where the leader has weaknesses.

Important tasks should take priority over urgent ones. Interruptions to the working day may keep you from doing the important work that will carry towards your strategic objective. Sometimes it may mean items are not completed as well as they would have been if you had done them yourself, but if they are more than adequate for the purpose it's alright. The leader must always remain part of the team and be prepared to make a contribution on the ground when necessary.

A simple and effective tool for monitoring tasks of self and others has been a simple spreadsheet to which every task is added religiously. It should be reviewed daily. In my own business, my PDA allows me to have access to the list no matter where I am so I can add to it when things spring to mind. This spreadsheet has a worksheet for every individual that I need to interact with and has priorities so we both know how important a particular task is.

This works for me and has been developed over the years to accommodate my preferences. I suggest you adopt some form of system to accomplish the same task.

Finally, the way in which a leader motivates a team will always be related to style of leadership. Evaluate what kind of leader you are. Do you manage your emotions well when you are frustrated? Are you a micro-manager? Do you have the right degree of tolerance of others? Do you tolerate too much?

If you are getting it right you will know, because if you are getting it wrong you will see negatives like low morale, high employee turnover rates, poor quality work and interpersonal conflicts among team members. If you see none of these, you will be on track.

6. Step Out

Sometimes when leaders are immersed in day-to-day activity or involved in too much detail they can get in the way. This stage is about taking time out to reflect and evaluate how productive strategies have been. A mentor or peer or a mastermind group of peers can be extremely useful in this respect.

Look at the big picture and compare it to your operational plans. How effective are your actions? How effectively are you using time? What are the results of decisions you have taken or are there decisions you need to take but have been putting off?

It is widely acknowledged that a leader ought to spend 60 per cent of time on big picture issues, 25 per cent on ongoing and routine projects and just 15 per cent on activities that are daily routine administration. It doesn't matter what the exact percentage is but the principle is clear of how effective leaders should be spending time. Take some time now to reflect how you are spending your time and repeat the reflection regularly, which means at least every quarter.

7. Systems

You must systemise your leadership process as the final stage in this leadership model.

Develop a habit of making changes one at a time. Do not move on to the next item for change until everything is right. It is quite easy to get drawn into developing new ideas and systems without fully completing each one.

This also deals with one of the major diseases that leaders suffer from. It is what is known as FTI disease or Failure to Implement. Ensure that when you make a decision that you know is based on sound business principles - you *implement* it.

There will always be elements of change, something to develop. A leader gets into the habit of completing projects and having wins under their belt. Start with little things – plan, implement, monitor…move on.

Always act consistently with the overall vision and be single-minded in your purpose, carrying through a unity of purpose into every decision, every project, and every action that is taken.

The Seven S leadership model

Strategy

Single Out

Success Monitoring

Structure

Style

Step Out

Systems

2 | Positive Set

A man was on the road to becoming a doctor in the US when he decided to move to Hollywood and write blockbuster movies instead!

At the start, he lived in near poverty in a one-bedroom apartment and faced the constant rejection of his scripts. His friends and family thought he was a fool.

But he knew he could do it.

Today, with three box office hits under his belt and a bank balance in seven figures, his self belief has been proved right.

Every successful person has self belief – they do not believe in failure. If things do not turn out how they expect, they make changes and approach their goal from a new direction.

Positive Set

"A belief in limits creates limited people."

Your focus is going to be a key element of your business success. Steven Covey, in his book, *The Seven Habits of Highly Effective People* describes how important it is, sometimes, to change your paradigm. Have you ever regretted how you have spoken to or treated someone because, for example, you hadn't realised the personal grief they were experiencing as a result of some kind of loss or bereavement?

This sort of sudden realisation of another person's hardship can serve to give us a perspective on our own lives. More importantly, it causes us to make an instant paradigm shift. Put another way, it causes an instant change of focus.

This ability to change focus is crucial. We must develop the ability to focus on appropriate things at relevant moments and bring to the focus useful attitudes.

Remember only 10% of businesses make it. Pessimists have very little chance of running any of these. The successful business owner is an eternal optimist; he or she has such a strong belief in their business that it carries every one with it.

Their positive attitude is continually reinforced by the positive feedback that they give themselves. The strange thing is that they do not experience any more success than the next person does; it is just that they are able to shut out the negative and focus on the positive.

Everyone can benefit from this positive belief system provided they are prepared to change their focus.

In common with many business owners that I have interviewed over the years, I have had to keep my focus to arrive where I am. Ten years ago, I decided what I wanted to achieve and what my business would look like. The picture I created has been my guiding force. Although the detail of my route may have changed along the way, it has never ceased to amaze me how powerful my beliefs have been in creating success. Despite almost losing everything, having to liquidate a company, make redundancies, downsize office space, I have kept that focus and the belief that I would create the business that I describe on the next page.

The reality which began as a picture

By 2009, Andersons KBS will be the fastest growing and best known accountancy practice in Birmingham. It will have developed the foundations to grow organically to become a member of the top 50 accountancy practices nationally.

Andersons KBS will use many varied strategies to attract and maintain the type of clients, known as POGE (Privately Owned Growing Enterprises) with whom it wishes to share business success. There will be in the region of 50 team members delivering a unique service to the small and medium sized business sector. Other accountancy practices will look to Andersons KBS. Its philosophy and team will be the benchmarks for successful business enterprise.

The clients will be dynamic, fast-growing SMEs in growth service based industries. The aspirations of these businesses will mirror those of Andersons KBS. They will be partners with Andersons KBS in achieving success.

The practice will be famous for its revolutionary and unrivalled service. Clients will praise the innovative, commercial and pro-active business advice and appreciate the unique way that it is delivered. Clients will always have peace of mind and confidence when handing over their financial affairs to Andersons KBS. They will expect, and receive, the highest level of service, irrespective of the member of the team or the query that has been raised. A visit to the practice will always leave the client feeling pampered, relaxed, fulfilled and informed.

Every aspect of the operation of the practice will be standardised, guaranteeing the same excellent service time after time.

All deliverable products will be fully researched, upgraded continually and systematised to maximise the level of service provided.

The practice team will work closely, like a family. Each team member will be loyal yet ambitious, keen to learn yet commercially aware. They will always be seeking to improve themselves, to look for ways to make Andersons KBS more efficient and to find ways to pass on the benefits to the clients. The team will be trained in the latest technology and will be at the cutting edge of delivering solutions to the clients.

The practice will present consistently a professional, aware, fresh, honest, confident and clean-cut image. This will be true of every interaction, from telephone calls, to literature, from the offices to the team. This image will help to synergise the holistic treatment that the business shares with all the stakeholders of its success.

The value of making a commitment

An apparently rash statement I made once at a seminar I was delivering to a solicitors' practice amply demonstrates the power that flows from committing to a vision. We were exploring goal setting. I made a commitment that I would lease offices in one of the most sought after and expensive locations in the city centre. I also committed to do this within one year. True, I had considered moving offices before this point but I had no idea how I would achieve this. However, I had an extremely positive belief system. Just for good measure, I also committed to doubling my turnover the next year.

The next twelve months were not easy. At times it looked like I wouldn't achieve either of these goals. My focus however always kept me on track. I achieved both goals.

It is time for you to adopt this positive attitude. Start by looking at how you can create that picture of your business when it is complete. Develop your objectives and keep your focus even in those times of despair when it seems unlikely that you will achieve your goals. Do not be afraid to dream but make sure you are acting on making those dreams a reality.

Remember:

A belief in limits creates limited people.

The next step will help you to start working on something practical which will increase your chances of success, and also help you focus on your definition of success.

Every business needs a vision of where it will be when it is finished. The vision must be strong and detailed enough to be describable in a vision statement.

A sample vision statement has been included. This can be described in more detail afterwards but a few lines will suffice to set the scene. The vision sets the target. The mission sets the path to the target. Both are crucial to the success of the business success and must be rehearsed and communicated to all stakeholders.

An invaluable tool for charting business success I have found is to write a strategic plan. A pro forma has been included in the next chapter and you should take the time now to write yours.

Our Vision Statement

We aim to change the perception of service delivery from the accountancy and professional services sector. Awesome customer service, innovative, commercial and pro-active business advice will mean that our products and services will set the standard for how similar businesses are judged.

Our Mission Statement

We aim to become the leading added value multi-disciplined business consultancy and accountancy practice for small to medium sized enterprises in Birmingham by constantly exceeding our clients' expectations and adding value to their businesses.

We will grow organically and by acquisitions and mergers of like minded professionals.

3 | Organisation

The right business structure is crucial to success.

A family business comprised a number of different strands. Over time, the strands had evolved unchecked with the result that many parts of the business took up time and resource but did not satisfy the personal or professional aspirations of the family members.

The mother was interested in the training company, but wanted to cut her hours. One son was passionate about the construction industry and the other excited by the creative industries.

They took time out to develop a clear picture of what they wanted. This vision formed the basis of a strategic plan, designed to ensure they achieve their goals.

Every decision is now sense checked against delivery of the strategic plan. They have disposed of non-core parts of the business. The mother has reduced her workload and both sons are able to concentrate on work they enjoy.

If you want to reap the rewards of effective strategic planning, this chapter will give you some practical guidance.

Organisation

"Potter; knead your clay while it is wet."

The next step is to plan exactly what it is you want to achieve. Unfortunately, most business owners do not take the necessary time away from their businesses to plan what they really want.

This should not be confused with the detailed business plan that everyone is familiar with. What is required here is a live, relevant, working document - a strategic action plan.

Identifying personal goals and goals for business and how these two things fit together, is the precursor to preparing your strategy document. Only then will you be in a position to describe what you think your business will be like when it is mature. From this clear picture, you can then decide on the route that will get you there. This clarity will enable you to identify those actions that will help you achieve your goals and, those which will not.

Countless books, courses and clichés tell us how important it is to plan. We know what we should do, so why do we not do it? It is because we become bogged down with the daily challenges that business life creates.

People set up in business for a variety of reasons…to be their own boss, have more free time, control their destiny, have more money, make a major impact on the community, become rich…the list goes on.

However, most people find instead that they get into debt, work long hours, are underpaid, feel trapped by the business, feel lonely, lose the love for their work…and so on.

A strategic plan will help to alleviate these problems. It will be a constant reminder of the reasons for starting in business.

Exercise 1

If you take only one thing from this book - make sure it is this.

Stop whatever you are doing. Get out your diary or personal organiser. Find a date in the next ten days when you can get away from the business with no interruptions. Book this day out now and use it to plan exactly where you're going with your business.

Your finished strategic action plan should comprise important strategic goals with an analysis of future actions.

- Strategy - Important area that you need to work on

- Actions - Actions that you need to carry out

- Outputs - Measurable results as consequences of your actions

- Timescale - When you expect to see these outputs

- Required Resources - Resources that are needed to carry out the actions

- Success Measures - Measures of success that you can identify

- Responsible Person - Who will be responsible for this strategic action point

See example on following page

Strategy	Actions	Outputs
Develop new income stream	Research idea	List of possible ideas
Develop sales and marketing function	Determine what an ideal client is. Develop and educate customers and the team about our USPs. Learn techniques to measure marketing activity	Ideal client profile written up. Customer survey and employee survey completed
Develop e-business strategy	Update webpage. Disaster recovery planned for security. Internal communication and e-mail	Website. Disaster recovery planned and documented
Greater financial awareness	Decide on Early Warning Signals and KPIs. Understand management pack	Test on aspects of management pack
Administrative functions developed	Fortnightly brief team meetings. Re-introduce appraisals	Minutes of team meetings
Leadership skills enhanced	Board meetings started with monthly reports. Training for directors	Board meetings minuted. Training logs completed
Commitment to quality	Quality Marks achieved	Quality Marks
Sales turnover to £2 million within five years	Develop a functional infrastructure first. Focus on added value and high premium services	Turnover increasing by 20% each year
New offices	Look for suitable location. Define all characteristics required. Accumulate deposit	Centre purchased

Timescale	Required/Resources	Success Measures	Responsible
6 months	Project Plan. Decision on core skills work	Operating profitably	A Jones
3 months	Information and examples	Client lists matches ideal client profile more closely	A Jones
Web page 6 months rest 2 months	Website company. IT supports	E-Bus streamlining administrative activity. Taking orders from website	B Brady
3 months	Training	Business managed efficiently	B Brady
1 month	Time commitment	Frustrations with the team minimal	L Smith
1 month	Time commitment	Regular meetings with action points dealt with	B Brady
12 months	Systems and procedures systemised	Procedures enhancing business efficiency	L Smith
2 years	Aggressive sales and marketing plan. New services to new clients especially around management development	Profit	A Jones
1 year	Finance. Project plan	One of the premier sites in Birmingham	L Smith

Exercise 2

Take some time out to write your Strategic plan. The following pro forma will give you an indication of some of the things you may wish to consider.

The following 11 sections will give you an overall view of your business and provide a solid framework with which to acheive your strategic objectives over a 5 year period.

Strategic Plan

**For the 5 years
ending 20--**

Prepared by ....

Introduction

This strategic plan represents the vision of .

This is how the business will look in 5 years' time.

Contents

1. Company statements

Vision Statement
We aim to...

Mission Statement
We aim to...

Strategic objectives
Within the next five years...

Performance standards
Timeliness...
Relationships...

2. Products and services offered

The company will be offering primarily .... services in five years time.

The product range will be split up into four key areas as follows :

1.   Product A
2.   Product B
3.   Product C
4.   Product D

Over the five year period the proportion of work being done will be concentrated in areas 3 to 4. The turnover profile will move from 90% in areas 1 and 2 to 50% in areas 1 and 2 and 50% in areas 3 to 4.

3. Business size and growth objectives

In five years time the turnover of the business will be £ . There will be a maximum of x directors but there will be y senior managers / directors responsible for all the key functions of the business.

The business will employ q people and the direct labour costs will equate to 75% of turnover.

4. Geographical Scope

The company will operate primarily in the West Midlands. There will be some service delivery nationally in particular products C & D.

There will be strategic alliances with other businesses around the country which willl deliver services on a licence basis.

There will be a certain amount of work carried on over the internet and will be an emerging market by the end of the five year period.

5. Target Market and Position Statement

The client profile will be dynamic fast. These businesses will be anxious to make use of technology and run streamlined efficient profitable businesses.

These businesses will typically.........

They will be located in the West Midlands area and work closely with

Ideal Client.........

Customer Focus.........

6. Unique selling points

Quicker?

Cheaper?

Better?

7. 5 Year financial plan

	Key objectives					
	Now	1	2	3	4	5
Turnover						
Direct cost						
Gross profit						
Sales and marketing						
Administration costs						
Establishment costs						
Net profit before tax						
Taxation						
Net profit after tax						

8. Other strategic considerations

We will practise what we preach. Whatever we ask our clients to do we will do. We will ensure that we have tested fully all new services or products that we recommend.

Will ensure that by continual research and development maintains our position as leaders in ....

9. Personal objectives of the business owners

Would like the business to be operating as a systemised unit within five years. If directors were to leave the business for one year it should have grown and expanded without directors support.

Will always give back to his community and be an active and progressive role model.

Directors like to sell their stake in __ years time.

10. Crisis anticipation and strategy for financial emergencies.

Directors capital introduction?

Taken over by bigger company?

Review technological and environmental changes regularly.

Disaster recovery schedule

Build up emergency fund

11. List of key assumptions.

Personnel. How many?

Number of customers?

Average value per sale per customer?

Direct costs?

Marketing budget?

IT budget?

4 | Technique

Understanding the techniques required to solve problems can prove vital.

A public sector organisation was told by its external auditors that it was not performing, its management was not working and the accounts were in a mess. Today the same organisation is an excellent example of best practice.

How did it change?

The board was restructured and a new managing director was appointed. The organisation then stepped back and every function reviewed before procedures and systems designed to fix the problems were put in place.

It worked towards Investors in People to show employees they were valued. Functions like accounting, that were not core to the organisation were outsourced.

Success has been achieved because the organisation learnt the techniques it needed to obtain the right results.

Technique

"It's not what you do but the way that you do it. That is what gets results."

There are things that successful business owners do differently from the ones that fail. If only you could find out what the successful people were doing, you could do the same.

What they do is essentially simple. They have a systemised approach to dealing with all the key functions of their business.

They have a system for sales, a system for operating the finances, administration, quality, production… every part of the business.

You might think that this is an impossible dream for you, that you just don't have the resources. The answer to that is, in the short term you probably have only your own resources and will have to do it yourself. Whatever, it has to be done.

You need to wear different hats for different functions; because if you don't, you're doomed to failure.

An analogy

Assume for a moment that your business is like the human body and the sales and marketing function are the legs. What would happen if you chopped those legs off? In the case of the body we would be unable to walk or run. We would have to stay put. This accurately describes what happens to a business without a sales and marketing function. The best outcome would be that your business wouldn't go anywhere. However, when the world is moving quickly, standing still is really to go backwards. Businesses that stand still die.

When the business's legs have taken it to where it wishes to be, it has to deliver its product or service.

Continuing our analogy, let us imagine that the arms and hands are production and human resources. The hands carry out the working functions, which relate to the nature of the work; the product made or service delivered.

Delivery is normally the start point for a business. People set up businesses delivering the product or service in which they are experienced in. The cook starts a restaurant. The accountant starts an accounting practice. The artist opens a gallery. The problem is that, very quickly, doing the work becomes all-consuming.

Very soon, the activity, which is loved, creates some success. In turn that means that increasing time is expended doing the work. What has been created is not a business. It is a job. Often this job demands more time and imposes more stress and rewards with less pay than if we had carried on in employment.

How we deal with recruitment, training, and retention of people is key to getting past this apparent impasse. It is as crucial as the product or service we deliver. People can be the most valuable resource in a business.

Important as the arms and legs are, they cannot function without the key internal organs like the heart. Imagine that the heart is the finance and administration function. If the human heart is stabbed, death from bleeding follows quickly. Neglecting finance and administration functions has exactly the same effect.

A very high percentage of failed businesses were once profitable, growing companies delivering excellent products and services. In many cases their problems were simply financial and administrative.

Completing the analogy is the brain. It is the home of innovation and information technology. Businesses must be forward-looking because the pace of change is so rapid. Maximising resources by using technology is not a luxury option but a necessity. E-business is about more than e-mail. It is about systemising and maximising relationships and processes. These include procurement, dealing and interfacing with customers and clients, the team and other internal and external stakeholders. The impact of technology functions on these and all other areas is a vital one.

In summation, it is essential to systematise your business, create functional responsibilities and to review and develop these regularly. Neglecting any one function risks the whole business system breaking down.

Exercise

Look at the following list. Do you have systems to cover all of these functions? Can you think of any other functions that should be considered? Read the lists and tick the boxes by the side. It will demonstrate what you need to do.

	DONE	NEEDED
1. Administration		
Systematise procedures		
(For example - ISO9002 creating a procedure manual)		
Answering the telephone	☐	☐
Receiving and opening the mail	☐	☐
Logging outgoing mail	☐	☐
Purchasing and maintaining office supplies and equipment	☐	☐
Faxing and e-mail	☐	☐
Dealing with incoming/outgoing delivery needs	☐	☐
Backing up and archiving data	☐	☐
General office security	☐	☐

	DONE	NEEDED

Order Processing Systems

Taking orders and recording orders by mail, fax, phone, or online ☐ ☐

Fulfilling and packaging orders ☐ ☐

Despatching orders ☐ ☐

Customer Services Systems

Returns procedure for receiving stock and customer returns ☐ ☐

Responding to customer complaints ☐ ☐

Replacing defective products or performing other warranty service ☐ ☐

Purchase and Payment Systems

Purchasing procedures and approvals required ☐ ☐

Payment process for supplies and stock ☐ ☐

Petty cash ☐ ☐

General Administrative Systems

Negotiating, drafting, and executing contracts ☐ ☐

Developing and protecting intellectual property ☐ ☐

Managing insurance needs ☐ ☐

Reporting and paying taxes ☐ ☐

Planning for taxes ☐ ☐

Managing and storing records ☐ ☐

	DONE	NEEDED
Maintaining investor and shareholder relations	☐	☐
Ensuring legal security	☐	☐
Planning and managing growth	☐	☐

Physical Space Management

	DONE	NEEDED
Maintaining and designing telephone and electrical systems	☐	☐
Planning permits and fees	☐	☐

Licensing

	DONE	NEEDED
Ensuring physical security	☐	☐

2. Production

Ensuring that our products and/or services are delivered efficiently and effectively

Product/Services Systems

	DONE	NEEDED
Developing products and services and protecting them legally	☐	☐
Developing packaging and materials like catalogues and brochures	☐	☐
Developing manufacturing method and process	☐	☐
Stock Control Systems	☐	☐
Selecting suppliers	☐	☐
Determining product or service warranties offered	☐	☐

	DONE	NEEDED
Establishing product or service pricing both retail and wholesale	☐	☐
Establishing re-order process for stock production	☐	☐
Receiving and storing products	☐	☐
Reconciling physical stock with accounting records	☐	☐

3. Finance

Ensuring that profitability is sustained
and cash and expenditure are managed

Sales and Credit Control Systems

	DONE	NEEDED
Invoicing customers	☐	☐
Receiving payment and crediting customers for payment by cash, cheque, credit card or other instruments	☐	☐
Initiating the collection process for delinquent customers	☐	☐

General Finance Systems

	DONE	NEEDED
Managing the accounting process with daily, weekly, monthly, quarterly, and annual reports	☐	☐
Managing cash with future borrowing needs secured and available	☐	☐
Budgeting and forecasting	☐	☐
Reporting taxes	☐	☐

	DONE	NEEDED

4. Sales and Marketing

Ensuring turnover targets are met building multiple streams of income

Marketing is the function that controls the image of the company in every detail wherever the company interfaces with the public and the marketplace

Marketing Systems

	DONE	NEEDED
Creating an overall marketing plan	☐	☐
Designing and producing promotional materials	☐	☐
Developing general leads and prospects	☐	☐
Creating an advertising plan	☐	☐
Creating a public relations plan	☐	☐
Creating a direct mail plan	☐	☐
Developing and maintaining a database	☐	☐
Developing and maintaining a website	☐	☐
Analysing and tracking sales statistics	☐	☐

	DONE	NEEDED

5. Human Resources

Take responsibility for recruiting, training and
motivation of employees
(Example - Investors in People)

Human resources systems

	DONE	NEEDED
Hiring procedures and contracts of employment	☐	☐
Training employees	☐	☐
Payroll process and benefit plans	☐	☐
Annual and study leave	☐	☐
Employee appraisals	☐	☐
Sickness and other absence reporting	☐	☐
Induction procedures	☐	☐
Company handbook	☐	☐

6. Information Technology

	DONE	NEEDED
IT Systems	☐	☐
Checking computer hardware and software	☐	☐
Using technology to streamline systems	☐	☐
Backing-up	☐	☐
Disaster recovery	☐	☐

	DONE	NEEDED

7. Leadership

Takes responsibility for making sure we are working towards our strategic and operational plans

	DONE	NEEDED
Takes responsibility for developing the business	☐	☐
Managing meetings	☐	☐
Strategic plans	☐	☐
Business plans	☐	☐

5 | Investment

A lack of funds is the most common reason for business failure.

Successful business people understand the resources they need and make sure they get them.

An entrepreneur with one fast food outlet wanted to create a national franchise. Since key to success was acquiring a number of prime sites, realising this vision required a lot of money.

The entrepreneur had already invested significantly, but the business plan also forecast large losses in the early years that needed to be financed.

The bank was persuaded on the basis of the long term vision and the detail of a business plan that set realistic expectations. The early financial losses generated no nervousness since they were predicted, instead serving to prove the credibility of the business plan.

This chapter will help you raise the finance you need.

Investment

"If you have nothing you are anxious to please."

Management information is crucial to any business. A successful business can only manage that which it can measure. It is necessary and important to have a set of indicators, financial and non-financial. They will need regular monitoring, some daily, like the bank balance, others weekly, monthly, quarterly as appropriate. These key performance indicators (KPI) are enhanced by early warning signals (EWS) that warn of impending danger.

By determining what the key drivers of any business are, it is possible to identify these measures for monitoring on a regular basis.

Exercise

Take a look at the following examples and use as guidelines to develop your own.

Financial Benchmarks	Non-Financial Benchmarks
Bank balance	Customer satisfaction
Total products sold	Quality of work
Debtors	Team morale
Cash collected	'Smiley' factor
% Jobs completed on time	Team image
% Unproductive time	Firm image
% Net profit on each job	Understanding the firm's strategy
Sales	New product ideas generated
Net profit	The life/work balance
Number of jobs invoiced	Systemisation (What have we systemised this month)
Average job turnaround time	The effectiveness of training
The effectiveness of training	The use of IT in the business
Clients gained/lost	
Employee turnover	
% time absent/sick	
% deadlines missed	
Number of referrals	
% of referrals converted	
Net profit per profit centre	

There are very few businesses that, at some stage, do not require an input of finance. Many businesses start undercapitalised and then find they are always playing catch up. Others need additional finance for growth, capital expansion or, in the worst case, bad debts, losses or negative cash flow.

Whatever the reason, the impact can be dramatic. Simply running out of cash has caused many businesses to fail.

Successful business owners have 'a good handle on the numbers'. In particular, they are able to ensure that their business is financed in the right proportions.

Before trying to raise finance, they will ensure that they maximise their own internal resources. They will utilise their working capital efficiently. They will not keep too much stock sitting idle or going obsolete. They will have efficient collection techniques to keep debtors down. They will pay creditors within agreed terms and conditions but not early unless there are compelling or attractive reasons to do so.

Once the business owner has ensured that internal processes are running smoothly and costs are minimised, then they can look to other sources of finance.

It is important to raise the type of finance relevant to your needs. Short-term requirements should be funded by short-term finance. For example, an overdraft is an effective method of helping with cash flow requirements, which come about because of temporary lapses in the timing of receipts. Trade Debt factoring may finance requirements for more permanent working capital. A good example is an employment agency, where employees are always paid before the customers pay their invoices.

Finance for the purchase of fixed assets should be long-term, for example, by a term loan. However, if a business is looking to expand, and the owners do not mind giving up some of the ownership, then equity finance may be appropriate. However, attracting it can be difficult for a small company.

Appropriate financial arrangements should be made for every stage of development. When times are good, money should be set aside for conditions that are more difficult. In good times, costs should be controlled as keenly as possible.

If a business is suffering from returned cheques, suppliers putting a stop on the account, inability to pay the VAT or PAYE, inability to pay the owners a reasonable salary…it is time to take decisive action, but not to panic. As frightening as they may seem, these are just symptoms, not the disease. What is required is a proactive approach and to deal with the causes. The causes of problems need to be identified and treated. If they are not, raising finance will just mean throwing good money after bad.

The following analogy may be useful.

Imagine you have a fish tank full of exotic fish. You are so busy, you never get around to cleaning it. It becomes dirty and polluted. Consequently, your fish become diseased. Fortunately, you have a friend who has a clean fish tank but no fish. He lets you put your sick fish into his clean tank and treat them with medicine. When your fish recover, what would be the consequence of putting them back into the dirty tank?

The moral is clear. Do not raise finance to sort out problems and then carry on as if nothing has happened. Treat causes, not symptoms.

Finally, depending on location or business sector, there might be subsidies or grants available. Check with your local Business Link and Learning Skills Council for more information.

Deciding on the best type of finance

Choosing appropriate finance for small businesses is an area in which the details of each case - current circumstances and what the business wants to do - must be taken into account.

Types of finance

The following are some of the finance options that can be considered. It is by no means exhaustive.

Grants, Overdraft, Factoring, Invoice Discounting, Development Funding, Bank Loan, Venture Capital, Guarantee Schemes, Lease/HP

I have found the following diagram a useful aid in understanding finance.

Deciding on the type of finance

1. Can working capital management be improved to avoid the need to raise it all through external finance?

NO | **YES** → Improve Control

2. Are grants available for this project?

NO | **YES** → Grant

3. Do you have a high quality management team or proven track record? Is your business profitable?

NO | **YES** →
Factoring if applicable
Overdraft if security
Term Loan if security
HP/Lease if no security
Loan guarantee scheme

4. Are you willing to share control?

NO | **YES** → Venture Capital

If you reach the stage of trying to raise external finance, the information you might need to use is as follows.

1) Business plan

Typical content:

- executive summary
- background report
- products or services
- management
- market
- operations of the business
- financial analysis
- SWOT analysis
- exit route and
- objectives and timings

To include:

- 3 years audited accounts
- Management accounts
- Forecasts to include cash flow
- CVs of key employees and directors

2) Personal information including assets and liabilities statement for directors

3) 6 months business bank statements

4) Details of any security offered

5) Good references

Examples of factors that a lender could consider:

1. Is the business profitable?
2. Are the assets of the business in good order? Will they need replacing in the near future?
3. Does the business have a positive cash flow?
4. Does the business have a good track record with lenders?

5. Does the business manage its banking arrangements effectively?

6. Can the business afford to repay loans comfortably? How much can it repay?

7. Has the business been refused finance? If so, why?

8. What is the management and organisational structure like?

9. Details of ownership and key-man insurance.

10. Are accounts prepared and filed on time?

11. Are management accounts prepared?

12. Are budgets prepared?

13. How accurate have budgets been historically?

14. Are there any current, pending or threatened litigation or legal proceedings?

15. What capital commitments are there, including lease and hire purchase?

16. Are there any contingent liabilities or off-balance sheet arrangements?

17. Are there any material contracts other than in the normal course of business?

18. Are there any transactions not in the ordinary course of business with related parties?

19. Do the owners/directors have personal assets/borrowings?

20. Is there any security/guarantee available?

21. What will the finance be used for?

22. Is there a business plan available?

If a business wants the maximum loan at under 2% over base, they must expect to provide a great deal of supporting, blemish-free information.

However, there are lenders who will take a view on cases with non-standard requirements.

Always decide what type of finance is suitable and make sure you raise enough for all your requirements. A useful shorthand guide is this:

Equity - to finance the risk element.

Medium to long-term loans - for core borrowing and fixed assets.

Short-term borrowing - for working capital.

Definitions

Grant	A source of money that comes from a funding agency. Usually contingent on factors like location, purpose and whether it will create jobs.
Overdraft	A flexible form of bank lending. The business only pays for the funds used. However, overdrafts are repayable upon demand.
Factoring	Factoring involves the purchase of the trade debts owed to a business by a factoring company. The total cost will be more than an overdraft.
Invoice Discounting	A similar arrangement to factoring, but confidential. The customer should be unaware that the invoice has been discounted.
Development Funding	Venture capital provided after a company has become established, to fund an expansion of the business.
Term loan	A loan for a fixed amount with a fixed repayment schedule normally from a bank.
Guarantee schemes	A guarantee on loans by a third party to secure finance from other sources.
Lease/HP	Renting an asset for most of its useful life.
Venture capital	The concept of adding value to investments by participating in the management and offering advice.

Now you have the plan. You know why you want the plan to work. You have the techniques and the money to do it.

How can you speed up the process of success?

6 | Mentoring

Everyone should have a mentor.

They can help you to keep going in the face of seemingly insurmountable obstacles, they can give you the benefit of their experience and learning from their mistakes means you are likely to avoid your own.

An advertising and PR executive set up his own business. His market knowledge and creative flair meant he was excellent at attracting clients. But the day-to-day running of his business was another matter.

With the support of a good mentor, he very quickly built the reputation of his company, a name for himself as a good managing director and attracted senior directors to the agency.

As a guide and councillor the mentor shared his experiences, helping the executive to learn quickly.

The mentoring relationship was two way, with the executive challenging the mentor and sharing his own knowledge.

Mentoring

"If you want to be great and successful, you must walk hand-in-hand, side by side with great and successful people."

As businesses develop, there will be a lack of relevant skills to take it to the next stage in many areas. Seeking expert advice is crucial. Although this chapter relates to identifying and developing relationships with mentors its primary focus is about getting help.

A mentor is a wise and trusted counsellor. Someone who has 'been there' and can be invaluable in helping create success.

Many successful business people were helped by one or more individuals to get where they are. This help can be as simple as an introduction or contact, a word of caution or a friendly prod in the right direction.

The relationship with a mentor is entirely a matter for the people involved, as is frequency of contact. It can vary from a regular phone call to a monthly or weekly meeting. Whatever, taking time to plan each meeting and consider what is to be gained from the contact will enhance the value for both parties.

It is important to trust the mentor's advice. I know someone who was advised to build bridges with an estranged business colleague. The advice was taken and resulted in a rich stream of contacts and referrals.

A mentor can help to speed up the process of creating business success. Most businesses go through several stages before they succeed in a significant way.

Stage one is the 'Survival' stage - just being able to provide your product or service, pay the wages and have a little left over. This can last for as long as two to three years for many businesses. What type of mentor could help at this stage? Ideally, it will be someone who has been through the stage in the same industry or sector.

Then there is the 'Existence' stage. The business yields a reasonable living for the owners but they have to work long hours and dare not take an extended holiday. Few businesses escape this stage. Those that do can take several years to manage it.

The stage is only escaped by installing systems, procedures and people such that the owner could be absent for three months or more in the sure knowledge that profitable growth would continue.

If escape is engineered, the next stage is the 'Growth' stage. Functional managers can be employed and the business starts to have a life of its own. Success is in sight.

Having a business mentor can reduce dramatically the time it takes to move through those stages.

To find a mentor requires deciding exactly what type of help is needed. This is best done by drafting a 'person specification' and 'job description'. Having the wrong type of mentor can be worse than having none. It can waste time - the business owner's scarcest commodity.

Next, a decision needs to be made about whether the mentor (or mentors) will be from a similar business, or can bring the necessary skills and attributes from a different sector.

Once there is a list of potential mentors, they should be contacted boldly. A good tactic is to offer them lunch and to explain honestly and clearly why you have chosen them and what you want them to do. Most people enjoy being asked to help and the responses are often surprising.

A more formal approach is the introduction of non–executive directors to a board. These can be retired executives from a larger company or people with particular expertise in an area that is weak like finance or marketing. There are organisations like The Chartered Association of Certified Accountants that can provide a database of suitably qualified people. Alternatively they can be recruited through recommendation or advertising.

Networking

It's not what you know – but who you know – and even more importantly who knows you that really counts.

Networking is another way to find a mentor but is an important part of business success in its own right.

Networking is one of the fundamental parts of any entrepreneur's business success. It can be defined as the creation of a network of people who, know, like and trust you and want to conduct business with you. It can be the determinant of the level of your business success. I have developed a simple strategic formula for developing efficient networking, which I have called the Party Principle.

It comprises five steps for powerful networking.

1. Plan

Successful networking begins with a clear understanding of why the reasons for doing it and what it entails. We network to meet people, this increases the number of contacts and the potential for developing relationships which can help open doors and help to promote our business. A common misconception is that networking is about selling. It is not that. It is simply an opportunity to talk to and help people. It is often referred to as, 'word of mouth marketing'.

When planning networking, time must be diarised for going out to develop new relationships. There are many functions to attend, especially if membership is taken out of a local chamber of commerce, trade association or interest group. There are also specialist networking clubs like the BNI (Business Network International), whose sole purpose is to develop networking relationships. Select and plan your attendance carefully.

To raise your profile and secure invitations to more events you could consider writing articles or delivering presentations on your specialist area.

2. Attend

Before attending, research each event. Get a delegate list. Determine what you want to achieve before you go. Make a conscious decision to enjoy yourself.

Remember that most people are nervous in new environments. If fear strikes, it can be minimised by making contact with people with whom there are things in common. These factors could be as slight as the fact that you are both in the same room, both guests of the host; you are both nervous, you both travelled to get there; you may be in the same industry.

Be bold and make the first move. Conversation will follow. This will be covered in more detail in the next step. You need to attend to be able to network. Make a decision now to get out.

3. Work the room

Inexperienced networkers believe that networking involves developing technical, clever business talk.

The reverse is true. Big business comes after small talk. Developing relationships is more important. You do this by listening more than speaking. Becoming an active listener will give you the reputation of being a good conversationalist because people like to speak about themselves. To encourage them ask open and interesting questions.

Inevitably people will ask you what you do and how your business is going. Make sure you have practised your response – 'Business is great but we're always looking for more'. Explain how you benefit your clients as opposed to what you do. Remember, in conversation, don't interrupt someone who is speaking, or give long winded speeches. Talking about yourself continually and not listening will generally kill a conversation.

4. Target your network

Be disciplined in developing the network and be in control of it. It is more important to collect a business card than to give one out. Your goal is to record as much information about your new acquaintances, add them to your database and to keep in touch.

There are only two sorts of contacts; those you know and those you do not know. The secret is to get the first group to introduce you to the second group. This is called a referral. In an established network you will be able to refer people to your contacts and will expect reciprocal behaviour. If people know, like and trust you because of the relationship you have built then there will be no problems.

5. You

Here are some exercises that will help develop relationship building skills.

- List the last four times you had the opportunity to network. Include the names of those networked with, the information you shared or received and finally what the result was.

- What could you have done in each of the above situations to make yourself more effective?

- List your networking agenda. What do you want to achieve from networking. List the five immediate steps you are going to take.

- List the things you would like to offer and the things you would like to receive.

- Credibility and integrity underpin relationships. Always keep promises. Under promise – over deliver.

MAJOR ERRORS

DO NOT under any circumstances do any of these

- Arrive at events too early or too late

- Get stuck with one person

- Have your mobile switched on

- Stand by yourself

- Gorge at the buffet table

- Get drunk

THE **PARTY** PRINCIPLE OF NETWORKING

SUMMARY

Plan

1. Prepare your plan and make a commitment to network

2. Remember everyone wants to do business with someone they can trust and like

Attend

3. Be alert and visible. There are business opportunities everywhere

Work the **R**oom

4. Make the first move.

5. Have an interesting and exciting opening statement.

6. Avoid the major errors

7. Be a good listener – let the other person do most of the talking

8. Build rapport. Do not sell.

Target your network

9. Ask people for their business cards. Keep in touch

Work on **Y**ourself

10. Continually evaluate and update your networking skills

7 Self

An ambitious man, with a background in the travel industry, decided to develop a business marketing hotels through the the internet to people in the UK.

To succeed, he had to first market his own marketing business.

Understanding his target audience meant he got the product right. He found the right hotels and struck good deals and so was able to get the price right. He then set about taking his product to the market and developed a low cost internet-based strategy to reach his target audience.

Today, just 18 months later, the business has a seven figure turnover that is growing fast, with a world wide client base.

This story proves the importance of understanding your target market and using the knowledge to create an irresistible proposition. Reading this chapter will help you to create a marketing strategy that will work.

Self

"The purpose of a business is to create and keep a customer. All business activities must be focused on this central purpose."

This section looks at the ongoing requirements of business sales and marketing in more detail.

One of the five most common reasons that businesses fail is because they do not understand the market they operate in. This means they market their products and services ineffectively and do not attract the appropriate customers.

Fundamentally, these businesses do not understand their own uniqueness.

It is important for every business to know why its customers choose it. The business should also be aware of the market - is it expanding or contracting and is the product or service growing, mature or declining? What is an ideal client profile? The business must be examined in some detail to answer these questions.

When this has been done, use can be made of some excellent information about sales and marketing. It is fine to be able to deliver an excellent product or service but if the market is not aware of these and leads are not being developed and closed then the business will stagnate. Few people are natural sales and marketing personnel and very few businesses believe that they are actually in the business of selling. In reality, every business is in the business of selling.

Before undertaking marketing activity it is important to understand what the unique selling proposition of the business is and to create a strap line to reinforce this message with every interaction with your customers and potential customers.

In our business, we are aware that clients appreciate the fact that we take the stress out of a part of their business, the finances, that creates the most anxiety. We give them peace of mind. We know too that they consider we add value.

By analysing our services and the feedback from clients, we came up with the following strap lines.

Knowledge Based Support (KBS)

We deliver!
Serious About Your Business!

Do the following strap-lines mean anything to you?
It's the real thing

Finger licking good

Helps you work rest and play

The ultimate driving machine

Finally take some advice from marketing expert Jay Abraham.

1. Fall in love with your customer or client not your product or service.

2. Stay flexible. You need to understand and appreciate your customer's or client's point of view and remain open to changing how you market to and service that customer or client.

3. Clearly express your philosophy to all three sets of customers you have who must be sold on it. They are your team members, your suppliers and those who buy products or services from you.

Do not rely on one source for sales. Make use of as many of the following as possible. When one stream dries, another can compensate.

Direct Sales, Telemarketing, Direct Mail, Advertising, Courses and Seminars, Referral Networks, Developing back end sales, and Endorsements

Exercise

Use the following questions to help in determining a marketing strategy to generate a never-ending stream of income. A marketing consultancy called *The Winners Edge* has developed these questions with original ideas supplied by the author.

Green Zone
Preparing the Ground

		YES	NO
1.	Do you have a sales and marketing plan?	☐	☐
2.	Do you understand the difference between sales and marketing?	☐	☐
3.	Do you know what the profile of your ideal client is?	☐	☐
4.	Would you like what the majority of your clients would say about your business?	☐	☐
5.	Have you conducted any research to determine what your customers would say about your business?	☐	☐
6.	Do you know the life-time value of your clients?	☐	☐
7.	Do you know what your unique selling proposition is?	☐	☐
8.	Do you have a clear idea of what values you want your business to uphold?	☐	☐
9.	Are you aware of the three ways to grow a business?	☐	☐
10.	Do you have more than 3 of the following sales generating methods in place?	☐	☐
	Direct Sales, Telemarketing, Direct Mail, Advertising, Courses & Seminars, Referral Networks, Back End Sales, Endorsements	☐	☐
11.	Do you have a sales and marketing budget?	☐	☐
12.	Do you know what the market price is? That is, the price charged by the competition.	☐	☐
13.	Are there any opportunities for premium pricing?	☐	☐
14.	Does a database exist of previous customer spend on products and service?	☐	☐
15.	Do you know the average value of sales in your business?	☐	☐

		YES	NO
	Yellow Zone		
	Sowing the Seeds		
1.	Do you have client acquisition strategies?	☐	☐
2.	Do you have specific, marketing objectives?	☐	☐
3.	Do you know how to target your ideal clients?	☐	☐
4.	Do you have systems in place to make sure you win the right type of clients?	☐	☐
5.	Is your USP woven into all your marketing literature?	☐	☐
6.	Do you have a call to action in your literature?	☐	☐
7.	Do you know how effective advertising is?	☐	☐
8.	Do you know what your current advertising spend is?	☐	☐
9.	Do you have mechanisms to prompt people to act?	☐	☐
10.	Do you have measurement principles?	☐	☐
	Red Zone		
	Cultivating Your Crop		
1.	Do you have systems and procedures in place to maximise your conversion rates?	☐	☐
2.	Do you have a communications calendar?	☐	☐
3.	Do you measure your conversion rates at each stage of the selling process?	☐	☐
4.	Do you have structured sales letters?	☐	☐
5.	Do you have talk guides/selling scripts?	☐	☐
	Gold Zone		
	Harvesting Your Crop		
1.	Do you have a set method for inviting a new client to your business?	☐	☐
2.	Do you contact your clients regularly?	☐	☐
3.	Do you educate your clients continuously?	☐	☐
4.	Do you go out of your way to deliver customer support services?	☐	☐
5.	Do you measure client service levels?	☐	☐

If you have scored less than 25% as a 'yes' response in any of the sections above you must stop and take a really hard look at the business. You have a lot of work to do and you need to start now.

Even if you are scoring over 75% 'yes' responses there are things you can do to keep these crucial functions working.

Conclusion

We started this book with the statement

Most people only try. I make sure.

I sincerely hope that with the information you have read, the seven simple steps will help you to become a successful entrepreneur.

The statement above can be used to remember those steps by substituting the first letter from each word for the ones in the seven steps so we get:

M - Motivation

The importance of this in achieving success.

P - Positive

Changing focus and staying positive at all times.

O - Organisation

The importance of effective planning.

T - Technique

Work on all the key functions in the business.

I - Investment

The value of proper financing and the dangers of undercapitalisation.

M - Mentoring

The value of mentors in accelerating success and helping avoid pitfalls.

S - Self

The importance of defining a market and a marketing strategy.

Each stage addresses one of the common reasons for business failure.

1. Failure to understand the market.

2. Inadequate capitalisation.

3. Not knowing how to run a business.

4. No expert advice.

5. Insufficient planning.

By working through the process, you can achieve success.

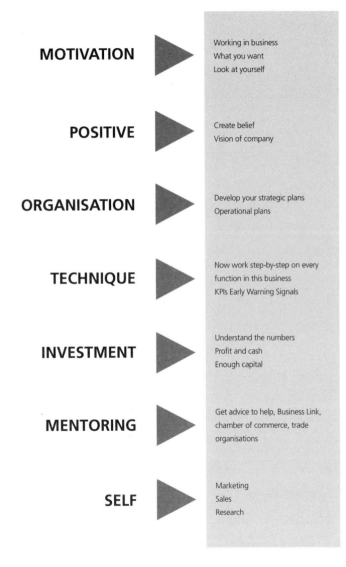

MOTIVATION

Working in business
What you want
Look at yourself

POSITIVE

Create belief
Vision of company

ORGANISATION

Develop your strategic plans
Operational plans

TECHNIQUE

Now work step-by-step on every
function in this business
KPIs Early Warning Signals

INVESTMENT

Understand the numbers
Profit and cash
Enough capital

MENTORING

Get advice to help, Business Link,
chamber of commerce, trade
organisations

SELF

Marketing
Sales
Research

Tasks

Now that you have read the book, review the main discoveries and take action. Many people are given good advice but the ones who profit from it are those who are prepared to put it into action. It is all too easy to listen to advice and think about taking action. Taking action is what really counts.

Start now…

1. Identify three things you have learned that can help your business.
2. Carry out three actions that will bring you closer to your goal.
3. As a result of reading the book decide to learn three new things. Decide now what they are.
4. Do three of the exercises in the book now. Do not procrastinate.
5. Teach and share three points with someone else. We learn by teaching.

Bonus Chapter - 67 tips

1. Put God first. Family second. Business third. Getting these priorities right is a prerequisite for any success.

2. Create your personal code of conduct. Live by it and let it dictate how you behave even when under pressure.

3. Set goals regularly. The more proficient you become at setting and achieving goals the bigger they get and the more success you achieve.

4. Become passionate about time. Understanding the preciousness of time is crucial for success. You spend time only once. Spend it wisely.

5. Get a personal organiser. Develop your system of how you record your time. Time invested in organising time will produce enormous results.

6.   Get a journal. Record your goals in every area of
      your life. It will serve as a reminder, a reference point
      and a monitoring tool.

7.   Work **on** your business **not** in your business. You
      want to create something that will give you time to
      enjoy the other aspects of life.

8.   Keep good company. The people you spend your
      time with should serve to enhance your relationship
      and your success. Make sure they share similar
      ideals and can give to the relationship as well as
      take.

9.   Be patient. Success comes to those who
      work diligently and it lasts longer where good
      foundations have been built.

10.   Sow good seeds. Remember that we reap what we
      sow, whether good or bad.

11.   Believe in yourself. There is a direct correlation
      between success and the belief you have in yourself.

12.   Develop yourself continually. Never stop learning
      new ideas and new techniques. Make sure you aim
      always to be the best at what you do.

13.   Read regularly. Leaders are readers. Make reading a
      life long habit.

14. Be persistent. Never give up. Endure the race until the end. You will get what you set out to achieve if you continue to pursue your goal.

15. Develop your business. Ensure it is saleable even if you do not intend to sell it. Have the choice.

16. Get expert advice in areas where you are not expert. Do not be afraid to pay for good advice.

17. Do what you love. This is a sure route to providing value to others and living out your life purpose.

18. Have a daily action list. Sort out your priorities and do not tick items off the list until you achieve them.

19. Put time in your diary to do the work that you have identified on your task lists otherwise urgent interruptions will get in the way.

20. Make sure all areas of your life are organised and in balance.

21. Do not take unnecessary risks. There is no reason to do so if you are working to a predetermined plan.

22. If something seems too good to be true it probably is. Do not be tempted into making rash decisions without proper consideration.

23. Stick to what you know as your core activity before taking risk. Research new areas properly.

24. Take decisions quickly. Act on them immediately.

25. Leave something on the table for other people. Whenever you do a deal make sure it is a win-win scenario.

26. Never speak ill of anyone. Develop a flawless character. Your reputation must always precede you.

27. Your integrity is your greatest asset. Guard it at all costs.

28. Your network is more powerful than your bank balance. Take time to nurture and develop it.

29. Have an emergency fund for a rainy day. Do not dip into it unless it is a real emergency. An example of an emergency is having no other foreseeable source of income for three months.

30. Make sure you have identified your exit plan for your business whether it is to be passed on to the next generation or to be sold.

31. Remember when the pupil is ready the teacher will appear. Be ready for opportunities that will arise.

32. Always have a positive attitude. This will ensure you focus on the right things at the right time.

33. Expect more of yourself each day. It is amazing how much you can achieve.

34. Cash is king. Make sure you have money in the bank.

35. All businesses are in the business of selling. Never forget this.

36. You must determine your end goal for your business and work towards it.

37. Learn to give. Be a cheerful giver.

38. Remember that people are your greatest assets. Treat them as such.

39. Don't aim to satisfy your customers. This is not enough, aim much higher than this. Aim to exceed their expectations.

40. Do not let your customers keep your money for longer than you have agreed. They are paying someone. Let it be you.

41. You will make mistakes. Make sure you learn from them. Learn from other people's mistakes also.

42. Get a mentor. Alternatively, have several mentors in different areas. They will accelerate your progress in business.

43. Keep your desk clear. Mess and clutter create disorder.

44. Employ people who are the best. Do not accept mediocre people. They are a reflection of you and your business.

45. Review your plans regularly.

46. Ensure you have the right systems in place for all functions. Employ the right people to manage those systems.

47. Learn the skills of running a busy company. Read books, go on courses, listen to tapes, ask other business owners.

48. Remember, life is a journey not a destination.

49. Plan your personal wealth as well as your business. Do not exploit your business but make sure it remunerates you fairly.

50. Make sure you listen more than you speak.

51. When you speak, make sure you know what you are talking about.

52. Take time out. Relaxation, silence, stillness, solitude are the words that should describe your relaxation time.

53. Treat yourself every now and again. You must enjoy the fruits of your labour to keep you motivated and in the game.

54. Do not be afraid to ask for help. There is always someone who can offer the right advice, contact or even finance.

55. If you get into trouble, don't sink your head in the sand. Take action quickly. Learn and move on.

56. Be passionate about your business. This passion will communicate to your employees, your customers and your suppliers.

57. Always treat people the way you would expect to be treated no matter how insignificant they may seem.

58. Just in case your original plan does not work, for every negotiation and business situation have a plan B and a plan C.

59. Control the way you feel. Remember peak state gives peak performance.

60. Eat healthily and exercise regularly. What is the point of business success if you cannot enjoy it?

61. Pay attention to your appearance and presentation at all times. It can sometimes make the difference between success and failure.

62. Ensure that what you say is what you do. Do not be a hypocrite. What you do speaks more loudly than anything you say.

63. Take action. Do not talk about things. Do not procrastinate.

64. Spend less than you earn, personally and in business.

65. Be bold but not unrealistic. Aim for the stars. You can achieve the seemingly impossible but you have to have the vision.

66. Take time to help others. Give back to the community. You have a duty to help those who come after you.

67. Do not neglect time with your loved ones. Remember, we are in business to create the security and lifestyle that we desire for ourselves and those we love.